Waiters

LEVEL 8

/er/

DECODABLES BY jump!

Teaching Tips

Purple Level 8

This book focuses on the phoneme **/er/**.

Before Reading

- Discuss the title. Ask readers what they think the book will be about. Have them support their answer.
- Discuss the book's focused phoneme: /er/. Give examples of /er/ words.

Read the Book

- Encourage readers to read independently, either aloud or silently to themselves.
- Prompt readers to break down unfamiliar words into units of sound and string the sounds together to form the words. Then, ask them to look for context clues to see if they can figure out what these words mean. Discuss new vocabulary to confirm meaning.
- Urge readers to point out when the focused phonics phoneme appears in the text.

After Reading

- Ask readers comprehension questions about the book. In what ways do waiters help you when you go out to eat?
- Encourage readers to think of other words with the /er/ phoneme. Have them write the words on a separate sheet of paper.

This edition is published by arrangement with Booklife Publishing.

5357 Penn Avenue South
Minneapolis, MN 55419
www.jumplibrary.com

Decodables by Jump! are published by Jump! Library.

Library of Congress Cataloging-in-Publication Data is available at www.loc.gov or upon request from the publisher.

ISBN: 979-8-88996-903-7 (hardcover)
ISBN: 979-8-88996-904-4 (paperback)
ISBN: 979-8-88996-905-1 (ebook)

Photo Credits

Images are courtesy of Shutterstock.com. With thanks to Getty Images, Thinkstock Photo and iStockphoto. Cover – garetsworkshop. 3 – RagabGamal, Africa Studio, Prostock-studio, Monkey Business Images, Stokkete, SeventyFour. 4–5 – Pixel-Shot, Dragon Images. 6–7 – Kues, andresr. 8–9 – MDV Edwards, Dreamer Company. 10–11 – ESB andresr, SpeedKingz. 12–13 – Phil Date, DC Studio. 14–15 – Andrii Medvednikov, andresr. 16 – Shutterstock.

Which of these people have jobs with **er** in the name?

Waiters can be the difference between a nice dinner out and an excellent dinner out. They help make mealtimes go smoothly so that people can enjoy their food without being interrupted.

Waiters are the people who help you order food when you eat out. They help serve food after the chefs have cooked it.

When lots of people order food at the same time, it can get hectic. Waiters have to keep track of several orders at a time and make sure they do not get them mixed up.

It is important that waiters write down orders perfectly. If a customer has a food allergy, getting the order mixed up could be very bad.

After waiters have taken people's orders, they transfer them to the chefs in the kitchen. While the customers wait for their food, waiters may offer them drinks.

Sometimes, customers may wave a waiter over to ask them for something. Waiters need to be alert for people who are trying to speak to them.

When the food is cooked, waiters bring it from the kitchen to the customers. A good waiter will remember which person ordered which dish.

Often, waiters may carry several plates at once so that people get their food all at the same time. They have to be careful not to drop them or get their fingers in the food.

When the main meal is done, waiters may check if people will be getting dessert as well. If so, they will take orders again.

If people do not want dessert, they may ask for the check. Waiters then take the payment. If they served the customers well, they may even get a tip.

After the customers leave, the only thing left to do is clean up. Waiters clear plates away and wipe things down. Then, they set up for the next round of hungry customers.

The next time you go out to eat, look for the waiters who help you. Be sure to thank them for serving you!

Which of these items have **er** in their name?